MODERN BUDDHISM

BUDDHA'S ANCIENT TEACHINGS FOR THE MODERN PERSON

DEVEAN CHASE

1

THE SEARCH

You probably already know, on a deep level, that there's a problem with humanity. A problem that exists within every human being. In the past you might have thought that the problem was caused by a certain lacking from within, but as you read this book your understanding of unhappiness will expand. You will begin to realize the truth about its origin. This truth is the first step towards lasting happiness.

In what way do you imagine your own happiness? In the past, what has your happiness been caused by? In the future, what do you imagine will bring you happiness? Do you envision a single moment or person or possession that will make it last forever?

You've certainly caught glimpses of happiness. In the seemingly drug-induced state of a new romance, or the liberation of stepping away from your workplace after a long week of confined misery. In the gratification of obtaining that one product that will outwardly show your success to the world.

Can you remember though, how long these moments of happiness last?

These moments are fleeting. They leave you longing for more. They only serve to reveal the stark contrast between pleasure and your day-to-day boredom, frustration, and anxiety. Leaving you in search of another glimpse of happiness from more love, more products, and more freedom.

What happens to the person that spends their life in search of more love, more success, and more freedom? What is missing from the core of the person that craves these things? Imagine what each day feels like, between transient moments of triumph. Do you believe this person will ever be satisfied?

If you know that these moments of pleasure are fleeting, then you know that this person can never be satisfied. This person may die without having ever been satisfied.

The person in search of freedom, love, and success is searching for happiness because they cannot find it within. However, ironically, the person in constant search of happiness will never find it.

The more you search for happiness, the further away it becomes. Gautama Buddha says that searching for happiness is like trying to reach the horizon. As much as you try, it will always remain in the distance. A mirage.

This search for happiness only leads to desperation and misery. Down the years and through many lives it has only ever led to these two things. You'll always wonder what will be the key to unlocking ultimate ecstasy, and you'll become more and more hopeless with every key that doesn't fit the lock.

The search is not specific to you. It's a common thread between us all. Happiness is moving further away from society, as a whole, at an alarming rate. Today, we search for it more than we ever have before. Societies have been searching for happiness for centuries. Why haven't we found it? With all the miracles of the modern world, why is there no guide that leads you through this search?

It's because the search itself is the problem.

How could the search be the problem? If I do not search then how will I find it? Imagine upturning your home, flipping cushions, and looking through drawers, frustrated, looking for the keys that were in your pocket all along. So distracted by *looking*, so distracted by the *absence* that you couldn't notice the obvious.

Can you envision a life where happiness grows unconditionally inside of you, with no attachments, nothing that could take it away from you? Can you envision happiness that exists without your need to look for it in every person and in every situation? Imagine a happiness that isn't dependent on a person or a thing. A happiness that no one is responsible for.

I promise you that it does exist, and it's closer to you than you might think.

This book is designed to expand your understanding of happiness through the words of the Buddha. Your newfound understanding of happiness will naturally and automatically shed your limiting beliefs from the past, that have been preventing you from feeling the bliss that you were always meant to feel.

Why Nothing Has Worked

The self-help industry has profited billions of dollars because of your search for happiness. You've probably already noticed the endless number of spiritual leaders, teachers of yoga and meditation, drug ceremonies, and motivational speakers that claim to hold the answers. But if the answers are evident then why are we still searching? Why is society growing less happy by the day? These people and these methods, for the most part, mean well. But they are hurting much more than they're helping.

Some lead us so far away from real answers that they become harmful, leading to the indoctrination of concepts that will never be unwired from the mind. While the other teachings you hear from this crowd are Buddhist concepts at their core, they often fail to express the essence of the Buddha's words. They try their best to condense these ancient concepts and make them more relatable. They attempt to alter these teachings in order to fit their narrative. However, they often fail to help because the concepts haven't reached them on a deep enough level to break them away from the illusion of their own misery.

Self-help teachers of today are just conveying words. Words through the filter of their mind, just borrowed knowledge that they're now passing onto you to carry. There is nothing wrong with borrowed knowledge, but it must be understood before it's passed on. Whenever the mind is involved, there are bound to be mistakes. Knowledge is deceptive, it is in the mind, and it has nothing to do with intelligence.

I routinely see interpretations and quotes being attributed to the Buddha, however, they are utterly made up. It's not hard to picture that nearly three thousand years after the Buddha created a path to happiness, it has become muddled. The path has become more and more convoluted.

It's not hard to believe that you're still searching. The path isn't clear anymore. Today's inspirational quote is tomorrow's stale let-down.

Buddhism Today

Due to the liberty of countless minds over the centuries, even Buddhist monks are relaying tainted knowledge. They no longer follow the path that the Buddha intended. Buddhism is out of the Buddha's hands and it has become too organized. I speak from experience. My uncle and both of my great-uncles are Buddhist monks in Singapore. With their own temples, their own disciples, and their own teachings.

After the Buddha died, his teachings slowly became a religion. The Buddha had no interest in religion, temples, and worship. He was simply a truth seeker. He was against all ideals and against all idols. The world has turned his teachings into something they are not. They have placed arbitrary rules and supernatural embellishments upon them that do nothing to further the interests of mankind.

The more you dive into the rabbit hole of misinformation, misconstrued wisdom, and diversion, the more desperate you'll become. Your anxiety will rise because nothing will work. The negative feelings will arise and the thoughts of despair.

"Am I ever going to be happy? Will I continue the endless search until my death?"

What you're left with, even if you no longer realize it, is distrust, disinterest, impatience, misery, and anger. These feelings, after they've boiled over and nothing has been done about them, merge into your being and lead to unhappiness and complacency.

Happiness consistently remains far from your grasp, all the way until your death. Then the cycle begins again.

Even if there were a possibility that these teachings could be perfectly translated through centuries of distorted language, they would still require a more modern interpretation for a more modern world. You could imagine that Siddhartha Gautama, or the Buddha as you know him, attained enlightenment under circumstances vastly different than your own. In a time of mercenaries, thieves, and sword-wielding warriors.

A time before the birth of Cleopatra, Socrates, and even Jesus Christ himself. A time so ancient that it's nearly impossible to imagine. The path to his enlightenment was not disrupted by the modern concerns that are experienced in today's age. Therefore a **modern interpretation during an age of modern misery is essential.**

The Absolute Truth

After years of searching, just as we have, the Buddha came to realize an absolute truth. When someone realizes this truth on the deepest level, their entire being is transformed.

The one who realizes this truth is the happiest person in the world. They are free from obsession, worries, and troubles. They don't brood over the future or live in the shadow of the past. They appreciate and experience each moment in its purest sense. They are free of anxiety, selfish desire, hatred, pride, and conceit. They're brimming with love, compassion, and ultimate pleasure.

There is no defined amount of mere self-reflection, meditation, mantras, or yoga classes that will lead you to this truth. One way to find this truth is through the words of the Buddha. He laid out a path, a logical, step-by-step path. A path to true inner peace. This path has been contorted and detoured for long enough. It's time it's been set straight.

In this book, I will show you the true words of Siddhartha Gautama, the Buddha, through the eyes of a person who has walked on the same path. An interpretation of the truth, formed for the modern person, by the modern person.

I can't promise that you will be ready for this experience. I can't promise that this will be the book that will end your search. However, by the end of this book, I can promise you one thing. That you will be moved, naturally, to experience the path for yourself.

A Wordless Phenomenon

Before you read any further, it is important to understand that what can be said in words can never fully express a wordless phenomenon. A state of bliss has no words, but it is only through words that any enlightened person has been able to lead anyone towards it.

The Buddha is not the only one to have used his words to create a path to happiness, although now we are exploring the path that was specific to the Buddha. This is not a commentary on the words that Buddha used. Commenting on words would only further dilute an already diluted explanation of something that can hardly be expressed with words.

Through a deep knowing and experience of the path, this is a repackaging for the modern person. Other times you may have heard a story of a certain place that was told to you second hand. That person heard the story from someone who heard the story from someone else. Much can be lost this way, like a game of telephone. Less of the essence will be lost, and more of the insight will be gained by hearing the story from someone who was also there.

2

WADING INTO THE FOUR REALITIES

In a lush, green, deer sanctuary almost 3000 years ago in India, the burning summer sun settled into the earth. The Buddha sat under a tree, with an unimpressive audience of five ascetics. It was only a few weeks after his enlightenment. His mind was absent; he was in a state of profound meditation and calm.

The five men seated before him, once his fellow travelers, had seen the changes in him. They sensed now the change in his aura, his lack of desire, completely removed from the world. They were eager to hear what he'd learned on his spiritual journey.

In that deer sanctuary, Sarnath, which would later be called "where holy men land", he spoke the core tenements of his teachings, starting with four simple truths.

You might have heard these truths referred to as the Four Noble Truths, however, I agree with language experts who have said that this is not a good translation. Calling it a truth implies that it is something we must agree or disagree with. The Buddha never asks you to agree with what he's saying. He's simply expressing his experience, his own path.

He asks you to see it for yourself, understand it and then once understood, respond to it.

So I will call them the Four Realities because ultimately they are connected to existence. Once these Four Realities are looked at, understood, and then taken into your being, there will be no room in your being for unhappiness.

The First Reality

The Buddha said:

Suffering, as a noble truth, is this: Birth is suffering, aging is suffering, sickness is suffering, death is suffering, sorrow and lamentation, pain, grief, and despair are suffering; association with the loathed is suffering, dissociation from the loved is suffering, not to get what one wants is suffering

Have you ever heard the phrase: "Life is suffering"?

It's a phrase notoriously attributed to the Buddha. Self-help teachers and spiritual gurus love the phrase *"life is suffering"*, because it can quickly form the basis of their teachings. Now, from this foundation, they can teach you how to grow past it. A student of this teaching could spend their whole life learning to get past it, fighting against it, feeling best when they experience short-lived moments of pleasure.

The Buddha never said *life is suffering*. This is an interpretation of the First Noble Truth that isn't just flawed, it's completely false. It's easy to understand, however, why it has such a stronghold in spiritual teachings.

Suffering is something you empathize with. At one time or another, you have undoubtedly experienced suffering. Can you recall a time when you were so filled with suffering that you were certain that nothing else could exist?

Acknowledging life as being filled with grief and sadness with only intervals of happiness is an almost comforting thought. It's a relief to feel that you're not alone in your suffering, that it's only normal. This is why the image of Jesus on a cross invokes such fervor around the world. As humans, we are very adept at empathizing with suffering.

Feeling relief in the acceptance that life is all suffering is not the way to happiness that the Buddha taught. This was not the Buddha's view of life. He was a great proponent of even the most minute aspects of life. He saw it as a source of immense joy and happiness. All he wanted you to do with his First Noble Truth is to understand suffering.

The proper way to interpret the First Reality is this: *"There is suffering in life."* The Buddha listed many things that bring about suffering: birth, aging, sickness, sorrow, pain, and grief, but he never included life itself as one of them.

What do you imagine when you hear the word suffering? Do you feel physical pain or is it mental? Is it the feeling of losing a loved one, losing money, or being discontented with your life? Is it an illness, an injury, or depression? The word means different things to different people. To some, it might simply mean discomfort, frustration, or discouragement. To understand suffering, we must understand what the Buddha meant.

The Buddha uses the word Dukkha, for suffering. It's in his original tongue and has no direct translation to English. The closest translation I have heard for Dukkha is *"the stressful, unsatisfactory nature of reality"*. To say it even more simply, *the unhappiness we feel in everyday life.*

What binds us all? What is the one thing that you're sure to have in common with your favorite celebrity, the Queen of England, and even Jesus Christ himself?

Unhappiness.

It's the bond we all share. Everyone everywhere experiences unhappiness. It seems more often than not. We've lived unhappily in ancient times and we will continue on this grand tradition in our future. We all live with, have been through, or are going through, *the stressful, unsatisfactory nature of reality*.

The Buddha wants you to understand this - because this understanding will be the foundation for his teachings.

Unconscious Unhappiness, the Modern Truth

Why does the Buddha say this? *There is suffering in life.* Because this suffering must be recognized. It must be faced eye to eye.

However, there is a reality today that did not exist much in the time of the Buddha. This reality is what I call unconscious unhappiness. This reality couldn't exist 2,500 years ago because it's a new problem in our society. This reality is something that keeps us far removed from unhappiness, unconscious of it. It is the drug called *instant gratification*.

The Buddha tells everyone they must understand suffering, but many people aren't even conscious of their suffering. Many people are completely asleep, even when you are awake you are asleep. You live in the eternal cycle of dissatisfaction, but it doesn't distress you in a way that you feel it in your day-to-day life. It's kept at bay. Life passes by in a foggy, drowsy state. Although you feel there is something wrong, you endure it, because gratification in modern times is always at arm's length.

Only the person who has become so aware of suffering will have the strength to move towards the truth of their being. Only the person who has experienced misery and sees the misery in their ways and in their desires will be willing to shed their ways and their desires. Otherwise, the person will see no purpose.

What's the purpose of making the journey to finding happiness when you can just watch the next episode of your favorite television series? When you can indulge in your favorite meals? When you can scroll through your phone, receive validation through social media, and imbibe until intoxication on your time off? There's enough going on to stave it off forever.

The world is intoxicating. There is blindness toward the present and an extreme focus on the future. The suffering lies submerged in your mind. In the modern-day, suffering might not be so apparent. It is there, however, eating away at you, affecting your mental health and your physical health.

If a prisoner doesn't feel the chains on his wrists or see the walls of his jail, how can they yearn for freedom? You will go on living in prison your whole life, your heart will always nag you and tell you something is wrong. But he will go on living without an inkling of the true happiness and freedom that is out of reach.

Become acquainted with this suffering, and become aware of the suffering in life that you experience. Become less distracted by your television and your phone and your friendships and your ambition, and become more aware that bliss has not touched your life. Become aware that if left unnoticed suffering will engulf your life until the last day of your life.

The Buddha said:

"'Suffering should be known. The cause by which suffering comes into play should be known."

The Buddha presents a task for you. The tasks he asks of you is to accept suffering and to accept unhappiness. To come face to face with suffering. You may find it harder to be impartial to your own suffering If you find this to be true, then first observe others around you.

Observe the complacent attitudes of those around you, the attitudes they have taken to deal with their suffering. The suffering they experience in their work life, in their home life. The suffering that they often mute with complaints, and commiserating with peers. The suffering they distract from with foods, alcohol, and material things. You are probably already aware of the suffering of others around you on some level.

Then look into your own life, your own mind, and your emotional state. Begin understanding suffering and unhappiness as it is personal to you. In what form does it present itself to you? Is it a clear voice of consistent nagging that you feel every day, or is it more subtle? Is it a small voice, suppressed somewhere in the background of your mind? You'll find how quickly you become familiar with this voice, emotion, or state, however, it presents itself.

You'll start becoming aware of the patterns that make up unhappiness in your mind and in the minds of others. Once suffering has become clear, you will be able to continue on the path the Buddha has laid out for you.

Had they ever crossed paths, the Buddha would have agreed with Socrates on one thing at the very least: *an unexamined life is not worth living.*

The Second Reality

The Buddha said:

"And this, monks is the noble truth of the origination of dukkha (suffering): the craving that makes for further becoming — accompanied by passion & delight, relishing now here & now there — i.e., craving for sensual pleasure, craving for becoming, craving for non-becoming."

The Origin Of Unhappiness

The Buddha said:

"People cleave to their worldly possessions and selfish passions so blindly as to sacrifice their own lives for them. They are like a child who tries to eat a little honey smeared on the edge of a knife. The amount is by no means sufficient to appease his appetite, but he runs the risk of wounding his tongue."

Take a hard look at the politicians in your country. Can you see how much of an effort they make to remain in office? Campaigning every year, involving themselves in dishonorable business dealings, appealing to constituents, and presenting thousands of plastic smiles. They'll risk their own integrity in a heartbeat to remain in the power that they've worked so hard to claim. It's all in a bid to retain that power, and they are all miserable - eventually blighted by the media, the people, security, and scandals.

Take a look at the rich. Do you see how much strain and stress they endure to remain rich? They've taken an arduous path to becoming wealthy and they only become more miserable trying to hold onto the riches that they've amassed. In fact, it's reported that more than ten thousand suicides were linked to the financial crisis of 2008 in the United States. Ten thousand people took their own lives once their money was gone.

Most of the people that come to me seeking advice are wealthy individuals. Unhappy with their life situation, wondering why their money has not made them happy. Most of them are on their second or third divorce. What goes wrong in these situations? Shouldn't passion and perseverance lead to happiness?

The Buddha said:

"Moved by their selfish desires, people seek after fame and glory. But when they have acquired it, they are already stricken in years. If you hanker after worldly fame and practice not the Way, your labors are wrongfully applied and your energy is wasted. It is like unto burning an incense stick. However much its pleasing odor be admired, the fire that consumes is steadily burning up the stick."

The more power people rake in, the more greedy they become. The more riches they have, the more riches they desire. They have become obsessive, amassing power, and fortune that can never be truly spent. They go on wasting their lives, paying attention to the wrong things, and in the end, they die, like everyone else, with empty hands.

The Buddha says that it's the craving, not the things themselves that make you unhappy. The craving for more than you have, more than you are. Craving for sensual pleasures, the things of the world. Craving for becoming, the furtherance of your life. Craving for non-becoming, the craving for death, the sleep state.

It is not just the very rich and very powerful that fall to their cravings. They are only the most obvious cases. You will begin to find that you have many desires of your own. Desires big and small. To become successful, to become beautiful, to become famous. Some desires are even altruistic in nature, such as the desire for world peace. You'll begin to notice even small desires such as a simple craving for new clothing or sugary foods. It matters not the size of the desires, only their presence in your mind.

I have witnessed many people, and you may be one of them, who become miserable with the state of the world. They find that they are unable to be happy while there is suffering all around. While there is poverty, corruption, and discrimination. It is partly because it is used as an excuse. They are aware of their own unhappiness, and it becomes easy to attribute this to the suffering of the world.

This unhappiness experienced is real personal unhappiness. This unhappiness is not caused by the state of the world, it's caused by desire. Altruistic as it may seem, the desire for a change in the world, and the desire for perfection create misery. The world will never be a utopia. There will always be poverty. However just because a person does not have what you have, doesn't mean they are unhappy. Are you happy? You have what they have not and yet you are not happy. Does your unhappiness make another happy? It does not. If you could learn the path to happiness you would know that it is not paved with possessions.

If you could learn the path you could help others on their path. In fact, your "altruistic" unhappiness is not happiness at all. It is pity. Pity has never been a gift to anyone.

Now, many religions and philosophies around the world believe in the idea that life is unsatisfactory. It's nothing unique to the Buddha. What is unique to the Buddha, however, is the idea that all suffering and unhappiness have one single source.

This is the Second Reality of the Buddha. All unhappiness, suffering, stress, and dissatisfaction come from one source. The source is of craving. This is your constant clinging, your obsessions, your desire for more.

The Buddha said:

If this sticky, uncouth craving
overcomes you in the world,
your sorrows grow like wild grass
after rain.
If, in the world, you overcome
this uncouth craving, hard to escape,
sorrows roll off you,
like water beads off
a lotus.

How is it that desire causes suffering? You must understand that for yourself. The Buddha's path is a personal journey, something experiential as well as existential. In your life, start to become conscious of your desires. What desires do you have for your future? What desires arise in you throughout each day? What things do you yearn for, and what do you observe in others' lives that you desire?

These can be simple and they can be complex. You could desire simply that the weather will not be rainy tomorrow, and when it starts to rain your emotional state will change. You can desire for success in the next two years, and when that two-year mark gets closer and you haven't attained anything, your suffering will be profound.

The Buddha said:

"From the passions arise worry, and from worry arises fear. Away with the passions, and no fear, no worry."

Start to become aware of your desires, become aware of the emotional state of being in desire. You might have believed that being in the state of desire was propelling you into bliss, however, it was not. Your desire is a restlessness. Your desire is a dream, a projection of yourself into the future. It is telling yourself that right here with what you have now is not enough. That you must escape as quickly as you can to a time where your desire is fulfilled. This escape can only be to the past or the future, so you will remain miserable in the present.

Your desires, big and small, will constantly trap you in the idea that your presence is not enough. They will trick you into believing that something needs to be obtained in order for you to feel bliss.

Until you recognize that the fulfillment of the desire will never result in bliss, then you will remain in this trap. When you recognize that bliss only exists in a fully present and relaxed state that is free of worry and desire, then your desires will drop.

The Buddha said that holding onto these desires is like holding onto colored rocks. When you discover diamonds, you will simply drop the colored rocks. They will pale in comparison to inner bliss which is like a diamond compared to the dull rocks that are your desires.

All Craving Is Equal

The Buddha said:

"From the passions arises worry, and from worry arises fear. Away with the passions, and no fear, no worry."

It is completely irrelevant what you crave for. Many people have grown defensive towards the idea that desire can cause suffering. They've tried to argue this with me, to put craving and desiring in a positive light. If the subject of their desire will benefit others, they feel that it can't cause them suffering. Yet it can.

To desire a more peaceful world is a symptom of the anger and dissatisfaction you have towards the present time. You cling to this desire as if it's creating a better world. Only actions can create change. Your clinging to the desire is merely clinging to anger and despair. Craving and desiring itself is the problem, not what you crave. Changing the subject of your desire to a noble endeavor might make you feel better for a short time, but it will end the same. Even if your desire is fulfilled, there will always be another more noble desire. You'll remain in an endless state of despair until the world is perfect. This day will never come.

Most religious people follow the same route. They fall into the same trap. You start by craving worldly things like money, power, and prestige. After accumulating enough money and prestige, or failing to do so, you come to realize that you never attained the bliss that you expected to come along with your journey. From this realization, you choose a spiritual path. Many people remain at this point. In a deep desire for divine bliss and wisdom. Immensely frustrated because it's all that they desire. They've renounced everything else because no material pleasure can quench this thirst. Little do they realize that it is the desire for the divine that is preventing them from experiencing it. At least money and prestige you might have been able to attain, but now you are craving the divine!

This state of tense desire, this strain to be in the place where they are happy. Remaining in this state is a trap that you must be aware of in order to escape. This is a worse state than the stages before. In this state, you have recognized that all worldly desires will not bring you peace, yet your desire for peace prevents you from achieving it.

It is only once a person begins to drop even the desire for bliss will they begin to experience it.

Remember that the origin of unhappiness is the craving itself, not just the craving for the "wrong" things. It does not matter what you desire, it's the desiring itself.

The Buddha said:

If its root remains
undamaged & strong,
a tree, even if cut,
will grow back.
So too if latent craving
is not rooted out,
this suffering returns
again & again.

. . .

The Buddha says that craving is like a great tree with many branches. The branches are the pursuits of the world, money, power, objects, and fame. The fruits that grow on this great tree of craving are nothing but unhappiness. If you cut this tree down but you don't cut out the roots, it'll grow back and its fruits of unhappiness will come once more.

What are the roots of this tree? Ignorance.

It is the ignorance of the roots of suffering that continues to perpetuate it. The way to end unhappiness is to understand the cause of it. This is the Second Reality.

First, understand that there is unhappiness in life. Second, understand the origin of unhappiness. The Buddha says there is a cause for your suffering. Your constant desire. Having found the root, you may now be able to remove it. However, understand that the roots are embedded deep into your mind, with many branches, large and small. It will take effort. It will take absolute awareness of all thoughts and beliefs to remove the strong roots of desire.

The Third Reality

The Buddha said:

"And this, monks, is the noble truth of the cessation of dukkha: the remainderless fading & cessation, renunciation, relinquishment, release, & letting go of that very craving.

This is peace, this is exquisite — the stilling of all fabrications, the relinquishment of all acquisitions, the ending of craving, dispassion, cessation, Unbinding."

What image comes to your mind when you think of Nirvana? Is it an enlightened state where you're floating above the clouds in peace? Perhaps you get the image of a beautiful paradise somewhere on earth. Most people I've asked believe it to be an ethereal realm, outside of this one or not, that you get to once you've meditated enough.

Unfortunately, the Nirvana described by Buddha is not as mystical as it has been portrayed. But it is vastly more beautiful.

The Buddha said

"Nirvana is the extinction of craving. It is the absence of desire and attachment. It is the extinction of jealousy and hate. The freedom from conceit, boredom and unhappiness.

A person in this state is not anxious at the time of his death. They will know they have lived a life of purity, done everything that needs to be done, and knows nothing more is left to be done. "

This is the Third reality. The end of unhappiness, a non-struggling, peaceful mind, free of desire, is possible. There is an end to your cycle of desperation. The unsatisfactory nature of life can come to an end.

Don't get hung up on Nirvana. The grandiose imagery it accompanies. It is simply meant to imply a letting go, a breathing out. An awakening from your lifelong sleep. A lack of clinging to everything.

Life is like breath, you cannot take in more than you need, and if you hold onto it, you will die.

In the state of Nirvana, when you experience a pleasant emotion, you will be passionate. When you experience an unpleasant emotion, you will also be passionate. But it will not bind you. The passion will not bind you. You will not be a slave to your passion. Your happiness will not come from outside of your being, it will come from within.

Stopping Desire

It may sound very simple. Merely stop desiring, and there is absolute peace. There is pure bliss, enlightenment, Nirvana. In a way, it is very simple. However, we've taken the idea of Nirvana and placed it on a pedestal. We've made a fantasy of what Nirvana should be and what effort it would take to get there. The type of devoted and other-worldly being you must be in order to attain it.

This air of unattainability that's been attributed to enlightenment over centuries is one of the many reasons that it remains unattained. However, it *is* as simple as relinquishing all desires. The *difficulty* comes in becoming aware of yourself enough to even recognize all of your desires. Then becoming detached from all your desires.

Some desires are very obvious, and some are incredibly subtle. Begin with the obvious and you will start to become aware of the very subtle. One by one, you'll observe each desire that you've become aware of. Dissect your attachment to each one. Ask yourself now, what desires do you have?

Let's for example say you have a desire to be beautiful, to be handsome. This may not be your ultimate desire, however, somewhere in your mind is this nagging desire that you attempt to fulfill every day. In the way you eat, the way you dress, and the way you interact.

First, become aware of this desire. Recognize that it has roots within your mind. Now ask yourself, what is your attachment to this desire? What do you believe will come to you from the fulfillment? How will you know that you are beautiful?

You may feel that beauty will result in adoration from a lover. You believe that their adoration of you will make you happy. However, has adoration ever given you lasting happiness? How many compliments have you received, and for how long have they given you happiness?

Now, imagine how you will feel on the day when your lover is not nice to you. You will worry, am I not beautiful now? Am I not handsome? When a picture shows a side of you that isn't beautiful. When age begins to disintegrate the features that you found beautiful. You will be in despair. You will be frantic until you regain your beauty.

Can you see how a person's misery can stem from their desire? Desire places your happiness in the hands of things that fade. In the hands of impermanence. Sometimes in the hands of the unattainable or the unreal.

The desire for beauty was only the desire for happiness. However, happiness in this scenario was dependent on beauty. Therefore happiness will never be lasting, attainable, or eternal. Happiness is only eternal when it is stemming from your eternal being, attached to nothing. In a state where you've realized that desire for anything only results in suffering. When you realize that desire is futile.

It is to be understood, however, that this person could still engage in the same activities. Still beautify themselves, fix their hair, flatter their figure with clothing, exercise, and apply makeup. But the attachment to the desire won't be there. This person could enjoy their beauty, but their happiness would have nothing to do with it. They would be happy on a day that they did not feel beautiful.

If a person is able to do this, to unravel all of these desires through the understanding of their futility, they will find absolute bliss. This state of Nirvana will start to grow in them.

However, do not cling to the idea of this state. The desire for this state will only leave you where you started, again in strife, in suffering. The Buddha uses the word *upeksha*, absolute indifference. From indifference, you will not have the desire. Only from indifference can you begin to experience Nirvana, with the knowledge of its presence. The Third Noble Truth is simply to be understood. The presence of Nirvana within you.

The Fourth Reality

"And this, monks, is the noble truth of the way of practice leading to the cessation of suffering: precisely this Noble Eightfold Path: right view, right resolve, right speech, right action, right livelihood, right effort, right mindfulness, right concentration."

Nearly 3000 years ago the Buddha outlined his path to true happiness. You can imagine how this path has been diluted for centuries after his death, while he was not present to remove the dilution and concentrate back to his teachings. It's been analyzed, made simpler, deconstructed. However, there was no reason to deconstruct this path, it already was put into a perfect form by the Buddha and it's as clear today as it was before. All that is needed is an application of it to the modern-day.

The Buddha has given us the steps to ending this cycle of suffering, craving, and unhappiness that we are dwelling in. He calls it the Noble Eightfold Path, simply because it contains eight parts.

The Eightfold Path can lead you to eternal happiness. Even more than the happiness that you're familiar with, to bliss. His path will give you the power to naturally and automatically summon bliss at any time. There are thousands and thousands of ways, and teachers who will show you how to circumvent unhappiness. How to temporarily distract yourself or move around it. But these ways are impermanent. They are attacking the leaves and the branches of the tree. The ways provided through "self help" don't remove the roots of unhappiness. Sooner or later it will grow back even stronger. The Buddha approaches the roots of unhappiness and dissolves them through understanding. He digs into the dirt of the human psyche and helps you pull out the weeds that are preventing your roses from blooming.

The Fourth Reality is a continuation of the Third: *There is an end to unhappiness, and it is achieved by following the Eightfold Path.*

The Four Realities converge into the Eightfold Path:

There is unhappiness in this world and we must understand its effect on humanity.

The origin of suffering is craving, clinging, and desire.

There is an end to this unhappiness.

The Eightfold Path is the way to achieve happiness.

Understanding the Eightfold Path

Understand that the Eightfold Path is not a set of beliefs, laws, or a code of conduct. He was not interested in controlled morality. The Buddha never spoke in such terms. The path is a guide to a personal experience that you must have in order to find meaning in your life. The eight parts are road signs that will guide you into a life of bliss.

The Buddha divides life into eight parts. These are the markers on your map. They are only meant to give you direction, not dictation. The Buddha is giving you his experience, for you to have your own personal experience.

The Eightfold Path has been taught in many different ways. Ways that often fail to encompass the true meaning of the words. They bumble on with the philosophy behind the words and talk circles around each other, going so deep into the words that they've gone past the source. The Buddha's words should not be dissected and followed directly. The spirit of his words are what must be followed.

Why is this? Because in 3000 years, the world has undergone obvious changes. Our society is dissimilar, we don't live in the same way as the people of many centuries ago have lived. Your life now does not represent life in Buddha's time, so you will benefit only to observe the spirit of his teachings, the core, not the minutia. This must be understood as you take your journey down the path.

It is also to be understood that the path described by the Buddha uses his words. It is the only way for him to communicate his experience to as many people as possible. However, it is difficult to describe a phenomenon that comes without words, without the mind. Using words, it is easy for a person to make their own judgments about what is meant. Each person has their own filter, attachments, and meanings for each word. It is all too easy for miscommunication to happen between the Buddha's inner world and your inner world when words are used to communicate. Just remember this for now. As we enter the path, the Buddha will show you how to listen in a way that will help you to understand without false preconception.

The path is divided into eight parts. The Buddha only did this for your sake, to facilitate your understanding. However, the way is one, a culmination of the parts. If you understand each part, practice them and cultivate them, the path will open up in front of you. You will come to realize you've been standing on the path for your entire lifetime, it's only that your mind has been wandering too frantically for you to see.

3

THE MODERN EIGHTFOLD PATH

The Eightfold Path is meant to restore your internal world. To take away the habits that have accumulated in the mind and have clouded your vision of truth and happiness. The parts of the path are often translated into the English language as *right view, right intention, right livelihood, right morality, right speech, right mindfulness, right effort, and right samadhi.*

However the Buddha did not say "right", he said *samyak*. This has been poorly translated to the word right. Samyak means balanced, centered, harmonious, in line with what will bring peace. Not "right" in the sense of morality, having to do with right or wrong. *Right* is meant to be your natural state, before all that you learned brought you out of it. This is first what needs understanding.

What also needs to be understood is the time in which the Buddha spoke these words. In this primitive time, the line between morality and survival was hard to define. Stealing, looting, and violence may have been the only means for survival. Political correctness was not a concern.

It was not a topic taught in work seminars and classrooms. People were not raised with politeness and berated for persecution. Fame and popularity were not the latent desires within each and every person. Materialistic desires were not dangling like a carrot on a string, in front of everyone's eyes, constantly luring them towards something new. There was no expectation of high achievements, well beyond survival for each and every individual. Constant chatter and gossip through waves of the internet between people from all over the world was not ever to be expected.

For these reasons, his teachings are even more necessary. However, for these same reasons, his teachings must be reformed to fit the life of a modern person. Without this reformation, these steps will fall flat. They will fall on deaf ears. You will not be able to find the lock where these keys will fit into your life. The doors of understanding will remain closed.

For this reason, these steps have now been reformed. Although the essence of the lessons remains the same. Because at the core we are all still human. We are as human now as we were at the time of his teachings, hundreds of years B.C. Now are explained the same essential lessons, however, with practical implications for the modern man, and woman.

Interaction With Reality

The Buddha said:

Those who have passions are never able to perceive the way, for it is like stirring up clear water with hands. People may come there wishing to find a reflection of their faces, which, however, they will never see. A mind troubled and vexed with passions is impure, and on that account it never sees the way.

O monks, do away with passions. When the dirt of passion is removed the way will manifest itself.

The world is reflected poorly in your eyes. There is a distortion of reality in your mind. The Buddha would compare consciousness to a lake, reflecting the moon and the sky. The world reflects onto it, showing itself to you in all its perfection. If you've ever seen a still lake you will see the beauty of what is above reflected perfectly on its glass-like surface. However, the moment the surface of the lake becomes rippled and becomes disturbed, the image is broken. The reflection becomes distorted. You can no longer see the perfect beauty of what is above. The Buddha says that thoughts are the waves that disrupt the image of perfect reflection.

Your mind is constantly disturbing the surface of your consciousness. Thoughts of the past and the present and the future create waves on the surface, preventing you ever from taking in the still and serene reflection of reality. Each second of reality exposes you to its beauty and with each second the image is distorted in your mind. Because of this you never find reality, you never find happiness, you never find beauty, you never find the truth.

With every interaction you have with reality you must begin to slow the waves. Allow the waves to become only a ripple. Eventually allow the ripples to clear and expose a clear reflection.

When you read this book, when you read any book, your mind is disturbed. The past and your opinions have collected in your mind like dust. When you listen, you must put aside the past, put aside the opinions, and simply listen. Simply take in what is new. It is Einstein that says you cannot solve your problems with the same mind that you used when you created the problem.

However, this is all you are doing. Using the same thinking mind that created your unhappiness to solve the problem of your unhappiness. The mind must be stopped. The assumptions and opinions must be stopped. Look at the world anew in every moment. Your memory is of your mind. It tells you *I have seen this before, no need to look.* You have never truly seen it before. Not with all the waves that you have created in the reflection. Maybe as a child, you saw clearly, but it is too long ago to even remember. Look at the world with new eyes, hear with new ears. The mind that created the problem must be destroyed. This is **right view**. To see the world with new eyes.

It is simpler than you think. The mind seems to be a solid thing, an appendage to the body. This is a trick. The mind is merely a process. A process is not a solid thing. When you stop walking, where does the walking go?

You might say, "that's stupid walking is just a process, when I am done walking there is no more walking". The same is with thinking. It is just a process. However the process for you never stops, therefore you believe that it is permanent like a part of the body.

Thinking can stop. Once thinking has stopped, even for a moment the process disappears, like walking. The process may start again, but once you have realized that the thinking can stop you realize that it is no longer a solid mass but an intangible phenomenon. For that moment the waves will begin to settle and you will for the first time feel undisturbed and you will see clearly.

Finally, at this time you will take in what you need. The

old process of thinking that has created your misery will be stopped.

The Buddha says:

"Just as when a sugar cane seed, a rice grain, or a grape seed is placed in moist soil, whatever nutriment it takes from the soil & the water, all conduces to its sweetness, tastiness, & unalloyed delectability. Why is that? Because the seed is auspicious. In the same way, when a person has right view..."

The Buddha says that like a seed, with this right view, you will become auspicious. You will be free to take in what is pleasing and profitable. Now what you take in will only lead to the sweetness of the flower blooming inside you.

Without the disturbance of the reflection, you will see what is true. What is the truth? It can be told but to be felt it must be experienced. In explaining you can only be persuaded to drop the mind, still the reflection, and experience the beauty for your own self.

The truth can be experienced as awe, as boundarylessness, as bliss, as desirelessness. The truth is not an answer to why. It does not tell you what purpose you have. The truth is the reality that we are all without division from every aspect of reality all around us. Whatever existed in the universe before man, before earth, and before stars is the origin of all current existence. Without the corruption of any religion, it is clear to see that creation is a constant phenomenon, present within everything, and is a part of everything. The same phenomenon creating life in the womb creates life in the tree. The same substance that created the earth creates the man and the stars and the earth and every molecule that inhabits the earth.

The truth is that we search for God whether we mean to or not, however, God is within every particle. God is within you in every fiber of you. It is magnificent, and it is a mystery. It is a mystery why this world has such beauty. Beauty that you can feel and see with new eyes. With *right view* you can see this.

Intention and Desire

The Buddha said:

"To be free from the passions and to be calm, this is the most excellent way"

"Those who have passions are never able to perceive the way, for it is like stirring up clear water with hands. "

With waves on the water, you will not see the reflection of the magnificent mystery that is reality. When the waves, the thoughts, have settled you will feel wonder, togetherness, divinity, and bliss in every moment that your consciousness reflects the reality around you. Reflect fully, magnificently, without interference.

With this feeling of bliss, naturally comes desireless-ness. What is often lost, what fails to become understood, is that desirelessness cannot be desired. This paradox alone can create a lifetime of failure in you. I speak of desireless-ness only to show you but not to lure you into the desire for this. This phenomenon occurs only when the mind has dropped when the waves have settled, and the reflection is clear.

When the reflection is clear and bliss has a moment to

arise, there is no need for desire. Desire is merely a result of your poor reflection, your misunderstanding. You need to find bliss where bliss is not. However, your desires only lead you astray. Your mind is not wise. It is blind and dumb and clouded. It knows that it wishes to feel happiness but is unclear where to find it. That is because the thinking mind is what prevents happiness. It cannot know that happiness lies on the other side of thinking because the mind is always thinking, it has never experienced it. However, now you have planted a seed in the mind, telling it that it must self-destruct in order to feel peace.

Even with that seed, you will have resistance. The mind is also the ego. The ego finds importance in itself. The mind carries the past and all the memories. The mind is very attached to itself. In your lifetime it might even decide that its preservation is more important than happiness. That the constant chatter is more important. However, ultimately, this is your choice.

What is to be understood is that **the person who drops the mind does not drop the ability to mind**. The person that drops the mind simply has the ability to drop the mind, knowing that this will bring peace. This will bring about the ability to feel the beauty of the world and existence without disturbance. This person understands that all the desires for more than what is necessary for survival are futile. They may prefer one thing over another, one house or one person over another, however, they do not allow a desire to create ripples. They feel bliss in mere existence and are aware that desire is just another ripple on the surface preventing bliss.

However, a person who can drop the mind will still use the mind. Even the Buddha still used the mind to create lessons, to remember the names and the faces of his family and disciples. This must be understood, otherwise, you will reject the notion that the mind can be dropped. That the mind can drop itself.

When the mind realizes that it can be used when it is needed, it will be more likely to budge. It will be more likely to stop. Now it is nervous. Constantly moving in fear that if it stops it will be lost forever. It will be there when you need it, as walking will be there when you need it. Walking constantly is just as disturbing to your peace as thinking constantly. Both can be started, both can be stopped.

When the mind is stopped and bliss begins to blossom, your desire for excess will vanish. It will become futile and irrelevant. All that you will need is the fulfillment of only what is needed for survival. This is what Buddha calls *right livelihood*. The need for food, shelter, and love. These needs can be fulfilled. However, more than the fulfillment of these needs leads you into an endless abyss of desires that once, if ever, acquired will only lead you to the next. An endless cycle.

Desiring Desirelessness

When you experience the bliss in your pure existence, the desire for more will cease. However, this cannot happen until the mind is stopped. Otherwise, you will only desire the ability to find bliss with what is needed for survival. Without first the task of dropping the mind you will simply be *desiring* desirelessness.

This is what is meant by renunciation. However, this has been confused many times for many centuries. Monks will flee to the mountains in a show of renunciation of the world and its possessions only to spend many years without happiness. Removing the self from the world does not create bliss. Surely one can escape to the mountains for the enjoyment of the mountains. One can escape to the mountains when he realizes that nothing he possesses or can possess will lead to more bliss than pure existence.

However, with that realization, there is no need to escape. With that realization, the world can be enjoyed.

This is why there is such a clear division between a Buddhist and a materialist. A Buddhist will make a show of their so-called renunciation without the feeling of true renunciation. There should be no clear division. A Buddhist could be and should be blissful amongst riches. A Buddha or simply an enlightened person who has experienced the settling of the mind is the *only* person that can truly enjoy riches. So there is no need to physically renounce.

Renunciation should pertain only to the renunciation of the desire for more. It should pertain to the renunciation of the idea that more is needed. True renunciation is the renunciation of thought, the attachment to the thoughts in the mind.

When you have become blissful and content, desire falls away. The constant need to *become* falls away. You are enough. The constant intention fades away into a sea of bliss that is your being. You are no longer *in-tension*. This is what intention means. To be tense, to be against what is. When you are at peace with what is, when you are floating in existence, you are relaxed. You realize that there is no need to fight what is. You no longer need to control because you are no longer on the search for what brings peace. You have peace, and you know where peace resides.

Peace is the natural state, the state of reality, the state of existence. This is what Buddha calls *right intention.* When you no longer have intention, you have the right intention.

You will notice that you are always in this state of intention. Even in very small ways, you can see how this intention creates suffering. You intend to be at work on time so you are angry at the traffic. You intend to walk into the kitchen but you bump into a chair that disturbs your path. You're frustrated that something has disturbed your intention. In grand ways, you are in tension. You intend to have success, to become great. Every barrier to your becoming creates great tension.

You are always in a state of wrong intention. Even when you pray you are in a state of intention. Searching for what is not. Your prayer should be gratitude. When you drop the mind and you find your bliss, your prayer *will* be gratitude. You will feel silly to ask God for more. You will ask only to remain without desire. And you will not ask some outside force, a figure in the sky, you will ask your own being because within your own being exists God.

Now, this is where the mind tells you that this belief is against you. This is what the mind calls laziness. That is because the mind is a cabinet of files storing all the lessons you've received from an unhappy society, from unhappy parents. From the people who destroyed the bliss you once had as a child and replaced it with intention. You were perfect in your being as a child, however the parent fears failure. The parent does not understand that bliss is not attained through becoming. Through becoming someone, a success, many more people have become suicidal than have become blissful because it is not the way. They do wish bliss for you but how can they know where you will find it if they have not found it themselves?

They do not understand that a blissful child will be

more likely to have success than a child full of intention. The child full of intention will crumble under the weight of it. Some will succeed in attaining wealth, but they will never have satisfaction in what is achieved. There will always be more. The weight of intention will be a heavy burden on their lives.

A child who is taught where to find bliss will be more likely to find what you would call success than the child of intention. This child will find happiness in pure existence. He will enjoy the process of work and movement as it is part of existence. This is what the Buddha calls *right effort*. He will be free of the thinking mind, able to find creativity, and able to solve problems. The blissful child would be a revolution in this world. The child of intention is simply an extension of the parent, of society, perpetuating the same problems of the past. Perpetuating the misery of his parents and of his society.

Understand that when you drop the mind, laziness does not arise. The mind creates laziness. Laziness is exhaustion from the weight of intention. Laziness is the absence of bliss in existence. Without the mind there is joy and an over-flowing of ability and creativity. Letting go of intention does not create laziness, it does not prevent forward movement. Just as bliss is natural, movement is natural. Growth is nature. Dropping the mind means that you are allowing growth, allowing nature, allowing bliss.

The Path Of Least Resistance

When you move on this path you will come up against resistance from the society, from the parent, from the friend, from the lover. These people all store the files that you are attempting to destroy. They all carry intention and the importance that they've given to it. When they observe you creating change in your life they will become disturbed. They will mistake that you are moving further away from them, further away from their values. In order to move freely in the world towards bliss, towards the destruction of the mind, you must move cautiously.

You will try to meditate and the husband or the wife will become jealous. For who are you trying to change? Am I not enough for your happiness? Dropping the mind, you will become more aware. They will feel that you will become aware of the misery in your relationships. However, you might finally become aware of the love within it that was lost.

In your awareness, you might see that your actions are not pleasing to your body. You might become aware that taking in other animals is not pleasing to you, not aesthetic. In your awareness you might become more sensitive to the earth, you might wish to cause less harm with waste and destruction.

Then the family feels you are not authentic, that you are following trends and becoming pretentious. They confuse this because many people they observe are creating these changes through borrowed morality. However, this is not the case. The idea of morality in our society is not true morality. Borrowed morality comes from one telling another what is right and what is wrong. From mimicking the actions of idols.

The morality that you develop will appear naturally from your awareness. It will have nothing to do with your desire to change or your desire to appear harmless. It will be a waking up to what aligns with your being. This is what the Buddha calls *right morality*.

Unless the family and the society are also dropping the

mind, becoming more aware, then you will face judgment for your new morality. You will need to move cautiously through this or the society will coax you back to the mind where they are living through. They will crush the seed that is sprouting in you. To protect the seed of wisdom and to remain on this path you will need to create an environment where you do not embrace the resistance from the external.

Patanjali would call this Yama, the first step in yoga. It is often misinterpreted as self-restraint however it means to direct one's life energy. The path of the Buddha is much like the path of yoga. The paths lead to the same place. Both paths are arduous and few will survive until the end. Therefore it is necessary to preserve one's energy for the path, and not to divert one's energy to the management of others. You must learn to avoid the constant reaction to the outside world.

There is a temptation to feel anger and defensiveness. To react without awareness and contemplation. The temptation will lure you away from bliss. A fire in you is always burning, waiting to engulf you. Slowly you will need to dampen the fire. For every time the world tries to add fuel to your fire you must resist. The energy used to create this fire will be too great. There is nothing left for your path and you will be too weak to survive the journey.

The temptation to argue, the temptation to defend the ego, the temptation to gossip. This will be constantly present. As the mind slows and awareness arises your desire to react will lessen. However, society and the family will not take this well. They will urge you to participate. Your silence adds gasoline to their own fires. Eventually, the temptation to react will be too great. The natural urge to become unreactive will not be enough. A conscious decision must be made to avoid the temptations. To remain peaceful, to resist stoking the flames.

It is not expected that you will become unreactive immediately. It is not expected that you become less tied to your emotions right away. It is only necessary that you practice. This practice will be made simple by your need to remain peaceful. It will no longer become important to defend or to gossip. The more blissful you become the more you will wish to preserve your bliss. To remain on the path to bliss much fuel is needed. You will be unwilling to expend what fuel you have left for the fire. However, it will still take a commitment, a discipline on your part to remain within your bliss and without reaction.

Once you've created an atmosphere of peace around you, others will allow you to become more authentic. Once the family and the friends and the lovers have become accepting of your lack of participation you will be free to continue. Once they have accepted your new morality, your lack of anger, and your disinterest in gossip, your energy will be free to continue on the path.

Meditation

The Buddha said:

My doctrine is to think the thought that is unthinkable; to practice the deed that is not doing; to speak the speech that is inexpressible; and to be trained in the discipline which is beyond discipline.

How is one to continue on the path? It is the same way one begins. To settle the waves on the surface of your consciousness. This is not an easy task. To settle a wave, not much can be done. Patience is needed. Inaction is needed. However you have been blowing waves on this surface for eternity, and your patience is nonexistent. Even your patience has impatience within it. You have never known true patience because patience requires an indifference that you have never had. You have only ever had intention and desire. Now is time for no intention and no desire. It will give rise to a new meaning of patience. True patience is not patience at all. This is the problem with the mind. Within each word and within each action is the opposite. The mind can only know patience because it knows impatience.

The patience that you will need for meditation will not be patience, but love. True meditation is love. True meditation is adoration for existence. This is the missing ingredient that keeps the sweetness from developing in your meditation. With love, there is sweetness, ecstasy. Without love in meditation, there is a tasteless impatience.

It is an impossible task to prescribe this notion. I could tell you what laughter is, and I could tell you what brings me laughter however without finding laughter on your own you will never understand. Even looking for laughter will take away from humor. It will be too serious, you will not find it. I can only say to be relaxed, to be open, and laughter will find you. The same is for love in existence. Be open to this existence around you and within you. There is such extreme beauty and mystery that it is impossible not to feel love if you are open. If you have no waves on the surface distorting its perfection.

Forcing the waves to settle will never work. Touch a ripple in the water to stop its motion and you will create ever more ripples. Be patient. Love is the only way to have patience. Time spent with a lover is no time spent at all, it is timeless. There is no indication of time. Love takes you out of the mind that creates time. This is the key. Love takes you out of the mind.

Many people are forcing the mind to stop with the mind. This will never work. This is trying to stop the waves with force, and force can only ever create waves. You will sit and with the mind, you will tell the mind *stop*. This is only feeding the waves.

Do not become trapped in this foolishness. Forget about the mind. It is an illusion. It is brain waves and sparking nerves. It is not you. It is not your identity. You believe that the words in your mind are *you*. Who were you before language? Who were you before you were taught these words in this language? You were simply consciousness and nothing more. You were a mirror, a perfect reflection. The world around you was reflected into your eyes and all of your senses. You were an experience of the senses. These words are not your natural state. There was a time when humans existed with no word. Word has become a poison in your mind, a parasite draining the energy from your being. Draining the energy from your experience of existence.

Imagine for a moment the experience without words. A silent internal reality. Suddenly the exterior reality becomes prominent. The other senses engaged. This silence is what is needed. This silence is what can be practiced. However, it cannot be practiced with impatience. Nor can it be practiced in isolation of minutes per day.

From the moment of waking a person can meditate. When you notice the attention directed back in the mind, bring the attention back to the senses. Fully immersed in each breath, each step, each movement. Even each thought.

What is thought but speaking to oneself? However, you will notice that it is not. You will notice that it is involuntary, misfiring in the brain. A parrot repeating words spoken. An echo carrying sounds. The thoughts are an illusion. Not to be identified with, not to be mistaken for your spoken word. When you are hearing the thoughts, begin to speak to yourself within your mind. The thinking stops. Because all of a sudden you are aware in the mind. You are now using the mind instead of the mind using itself.

The Buddha says that only awareness is needed. Remain aware in the mind. A house at night with no lights will attract thieves. However leave the lights on and the thieves will be afraid to enter, knowing they will be seen. Leave the lights on in the mind and no thieves can enter. Remain aware.

This can be practiced more easily while you are sitting still. While the brain is not occupied with controlling the movements of the body. In this state, you will have the most resources for awareness. This is typically seen as "meditation". This must be done. However, you will never reach a state of effortless mindlessness, of stillness on the surface, unless you practice this in every moment.

The Buddha said:

You should think of the four elements of which the body is composed. Each of them has its own name and there is no such thing there known as ego. As there is really no ego, it is like unto a mirage.

Practice awareness of your internal dialogue and of your external dialogue. Typically you will speak without awareness. You'll engage in idle chatter and gossip. You'll fill empty space with words. You will brag about the new journey you are on. Avoid this. Silence does not need to be broken. Gossip and bragging are an exercise of your ego. To avoid this, however, it is only needed that you become aware. Become aware that this speech, internal and external, are creating waves on the surface. You will become aware of this as you practice. The desire for gossip will arise and if you keep the words away from your tongue then you will find that the surface of the mind will begin to settle. However, if you engage in the gossip, if you allow the tongue to boast through the ego, you will feel the waves begin to form and crash on the surface.

This is what the Buddha calls *right speech*. To refrain from boasting, to refrain from gossip, to refrain from idle chatter. To speak on what you have not known is to speak through the ego. Right speech is to speak only on that which you have experienced. Only on that which you have gained through experience. The fictitious speech will only cause a disturbance.

Many people use wrong speech to tell you about happiness. Many people are regurgitating borrowed information to you without experience. This is the entire self-help culture. Speaking on what information has been gathered but not on what has been experienced by the soul.

Awareness will create sensitivity to what is known and what is fictitious. Therefore only awareness is needed. The ability to forcefully stop the mind cannot be cultivated. Only awareness can be cultivated.

The Buddha asked:

"How do you measure the length of a man's life?"
The monk answered, "By the breath."
The Buddha said: "Very well, you know the way."

·   ·   ·

How does a person cultivate awareness? In every movement. In every action, in every breath. The breath is seen as the bridge between the body and the spirit. Without the breath, the spirit no longer exists in the body. Become aware of the breath and you will see that its activity is married to your emotions. They move in tandem. In anger, your breath is different than when you are at peace.

For the Buddha, it is the same. For yoga and Patanjali, it is the same.. Monitor the breath. There is no need to memorize breathing techniques that others show you. Simply monitor your own breath. For a week, or for a month, come to know the patterns of your breath. Come to know the pattern of breathing when you are angry, when you are anxious, and when you are at peace. Because the path between breath and emotions does not flow in only one direction. The path moves both ways. Emotion controls the breath and the breath controls emotion.

When you come to know what pattern you breathe in during a peaceful state, you can bring this pattern into any state. When you're anxious, become aware of your breathing. Bring your breathing to your personal pattern of peaceful breathing. Use this breath when you sit down to meditate, and use it throughout the entire day. Stay in awareness of your breathing.

However, awareness can not just be limited to each thought and each breath. Each step you take must capture your full awareness. Every sound you hear must capture your full awareness. Do not separate this from one part of the day to another. This is what the Buddha calls *right mindfulness*. This is what is meant by meditation. Meditation cannot be separate from life as it is in the modern world. In the modern world, we separate time for medita-

tion from the rest of our lives however this is not right meditation, right mindfulness.

Right mindfulness is a discipline because the mind is
very persistent and very egoistic. It is very difficult for the
mind to surrender. The mind knows that it can walk and
breathe and go about the day without focusing on any
action. It has made a habit out of giving minimal attention
to the body, diverting most of the attention to itself. It loves
itself, it loves to be paid attention to. It is a discipline to
divert attention away from the mind and onto the actions.
On to the experience of life. It is a discipline to divert attention to the senses. The mind will say this is boring, I'd much
prefer to focus on my own senseless chatter.

In this discipline, do not fight with the mind. To fight
with the mind is to fight with one's own shadow. It is point-
less. Instead, become more and more aware. Each time you
notice the body moving without attention, come back to the
body. Each time you notice that you are listening without
attention, come back to listening.

This is a discipline however you must remember to do
this with indifference. It is a paradox. Why so much effort if
there's no desire for an outcome? There is a balance to this.
You are simply rewinding, untangling. You are simply
unlearning the habit of constant thinking. You are allowing
the self to come back to nature, to the natural state of being.
If you were to leave your house, you would come back
home. There is no extreme intention, it is just natural that
you come back home. Some effort is needed, yes. The steps
you take will be some effort, however, know that they are
just small steps leading you home.

Enlightenment

The Buddha said:

Seeing the way is like going into a dark room with a torch. The darkness instantly departs while the light alone remains. When the way is attained and the truth is seen, ignorance vanishes and enlightenment abides forever.

Once you have arrived home, this is what the Buddha calls *samadhi*. In this stage, only awareness remains. The surface of the mind is still, reflecting only that which is. However, there are stages before reaching samadhi.

Before samadhi, before coming home, you get a glimpse of the stillness. A glimpse of peaceful existence without the conflict and torment created by the mind. This is what you will find through meditation. There will be a gap in the process of thought. A quiet space where you are sensitive enough to find peace. There is a taste of enlightenment. Those moments erase the doubt that you have had that your efforts may be in vain. Those moments of stillness contain the peace that you have been desiring through all of your efforts in life. Those moments affirm the realization that desire is futile.

You begin to learn what creates the gap, becoming in tune with your environment and the inner world. The state of peace exists within you and always has, but now you are learning how to access it. You'll come to find that stopping the mind is not an easy task. Many layers of learned nonsense need to be recognized and fall away for you to come back to this state. Many have given formulas for coming to this state, however, the way of each person is individual. The Buddha gives the eightfold way. Patanjali gives yoga. Lao Tzu gives Taoism. You will take in Buddha's lessons from his own experience, however, you will come to a point where the lessons must come from yourself. The self will guide you back to its natural state as long as you understand where to look. The lessons of the Buddha will direct you but the rest of the inner tuning will be internal. As long as the trust is developed. As long as there is no doubt that this state is possible. The first gap will begin to dispel doubt.

Once you understand how to create the gap for your own self, you will practice keeping yourself in the gap, out of the mind. You will own the ability to do this. There will be days that are easier and days that are harder, however, you will have the skill. You will notice what is creating it and what is preventing it. You might notice a desire arising that is preventing peace, and the awareness of the desire will dissolve it. You might notice inner chatter that is preventing peace, and the awareness of the chatter will quiet it. It will all be a result of awareness. However, in this stage, there will still be some effort. The effort will come in remaining aware at times.

The gaps of stillness in the mind will become more frequent, however, there still may not be bliss within the gaps. The gaps may just be of non-suffering. The mind creates suffering. No-mind takes away suffering but does not create bliss. Bliss, enlightenment, is born out of non-suffering. It blossoms out of the stillness. It cannot be said what will spark the bloom of bliss for you. It may be the blue sky, birds singing, or the feel of soft fabric on the skin. It might be the feeling of oneness with the world around you. But it will be a feeling of no conflict. The feeling will be that all is right with the world. The feeling of god, what the Buddha calls dhamma.

In Buddhism, there is no god, not a man in the sky to

pray to. For Buddha, there is dhamma, the law of nature. Enlightenment is a surrender to the law of nature. All that is in this moment is all that there should be. It is perfection, even in its imperfection. The mind does not like to exist there. The mind likes to rewind to the past of nonexistence and the future of nonexistence. The mind likes to fight with dhamma, and enlightenment surrenders beautifully and peacefully to dhamma.

You will begin to feel so blissful in this state that you will become indifferent to the idea of enlightenment. This is when enlightenment occurs.

It seems that enlightenment is accompanied by a pinpointed moment. However, keep this from your mind as it will distract you from your experience of samadhi. You might fear the moment or anticipate the moment and it will distract you. Simply stay with your experience of acceptance of dhamma. If a time comes when you experience the moment, this is good. However, even then it will be no different.

People ask me, what comes after enlightenment? The same that came before it. Meditation. You will remain in your meditation with peace and with bliss because you will know exactly how to stay in meditation. You will be so skilled and so practiced at staying in the gap between thoughts that there will be no more effort. You will become so attuned to this state that you will not need to leave, and you will know always of its existence.

Now when you use the mind, it will be as a tool. The mind will not use you. Even an enlightened person uses the mind. The Buddha used the mind to write his sutras. However, when he is done with the mind he puts it away. The process is dropped. When he uses the mind it is not like you use the mind. It is used with awareness. It does not create waves and ripples that distort the surface. The mind is used carefully and avoids disturbing the peaceful surface. And then it stops.

You might now desire this state. In a way the desire is good. It is leading you to make the efforts, to start on the path. However, realize that desire is also a barrier. The mind is always searching and achieving. Once you realize that all of your fulfilled desires have not led to happiness, you will desire enlightenment. This is the last desire to rid yourself of. You cannot desire enlightenment because it is something you already have, you are just unaware. You are too distracted to feel it. To desire, it is simply another distraction. Another wave on the surface of your mind. There is no need to desire what is already there. All of your life you've been fighting with dhamma because you want to feel bliss. You want to control the surroundings to feel happiness. However, you don't realize why you do this. Once you realize that bliss already exists, only when you are accepting of what is, you will let go. You will be enlightened. There is no need to desire this, only to become aware of this. Then there is samadhi, then there is bliss.

The last step in the eightfold path is *right samadhi.* If there is right samadhi, there is a wrong samadhi. The Buddha says to be in right samadhi. In this enlightened state, you are aware. You are living in this world with awareness. This can be done in other ways. Some have taken samadhi to an extreme point, the opposite of what Buddha means by *samyak* or "right". Samyak means in harmony, and an extreme state is not in harmony.

There are people who avoid life and remain removed in a blissful and unconscious state. This is even revered in some places, these people being seen as holy people. However, the Buddha warns against this. Removing yourself from life in order to be unconscious in samadhi is not *right,* it is not in harmony. The Buddha wishes for you to be blissful and be within the world, finally now in samadhi, enjoying the life that was meant for you to experience. It is tempting when you find bliss to then be removed. To delve further into bliss and be unbothered with all of life, however, then you miss all of life. To be in right samadhi you are experiencing bliss in all of life.

4

_____

YOUR OWN PATH

The Buddha said:

Those who are following the way should behave like a piece of timber which is drifting along a stream. If the log is neither held by the banks, nor seized by men, nor obstructed by the gods, nor kept in the whirlpool, nor itself goes to decay, I assure you that this log will finally reach the ocean. If monks walking on the way are neither tempted by the passions, nor led astray by some evil influences, but steadily pursue their course for nirvana, I assure you that these monks will finally attain enlightenment.

Many, thousands and thousands, have heard words like these before. It is an ancient wisdom, not owned even by the Buddha. However, the essence of the wisdom is lost on those who wish only to accumulate knowledge. Knowledge will do nothing but feed your ego. Your ego being of the mind, will only bring you more unhappiness. This will only grow your attachment to the mind. You'll use the wisdom as knowledge to stack on a bookshelf or to converse on.

However, the person who truly needs to fall away from misery will use wisdom as more than knowledge. The separation between wisdom and knowledge is experience. The separation is discipline. Just reading words will not create the change to bring bliss. It can plant a seed if you are ready for that seed to grow. But only your readiness and willingness to drop desire and to drop the mind will create a change in you. That change will allow for bliss. But not words.

An effort is needed to make the change. This seems strange as you would think after all that meditation is not doing. The paradox is that for you, not doing will take effort. Creating awareness in each moment will take effort. Coming to know the teachings of enlightened people will take effort. It will take a great deal of discipline to recognize that all of your desires are not leading you to ultimate bliss. For some, many years. However, for others, it has been spontaneous. It can't be known. Although you will need to recognize the futility of all of your efforts.

Then a time will come when the effort stops. When you've done all that you can do. When you've learned all that you can learn. When you've tried all that you can try. Then you stop following those who have had their own experience and start sensing your own body and your own internal self. The rest of the way can't be shown to you by anyone but yourself. At that point, your mind will be quiet enough to hear the spirit.

At that time you realize that you must drop even your desire for samadhi. You'll realize that all your efforts have been in an effort to attain it. Now, these efforts are carried on effortlessly. They happen automatically as they have become your habits. They have become what feels good. Then you are floating on the river towards samadhi. This is when it happens.

Samadhi, enlightenment, nirvana, and bliss, is all seen as an unattainable realm. If it was not able to be attained, then the Buddha would not have tried as he did. He admits that there is effort, that some might not prevail. However, ultimately it is so difficult because it is so simple. The mind cannot understand simple, it is too complex. And you are attempting to use the mind to rid yourself of the mind. You are using effort to have no effort. You are using your desire to bring you to desirelessness. It is a paradox, and the mind would like only logic. It is difficult, yet it is simple. Try to see it as both. Understand that much discipline is needed because it is difficult. Yet understand that it is also simple, so that you may attain it yourself. You must see the attainability of bliss. It is your nature. The nature that you have been led away from. However, it is there waiting for you.

You must understand that there is nothing else that brings lasting bliss. Ultimate bliss does not come from vision boards and supplements as the self-help industry would like you to believe. They are creating an endless cycle of excitement and misery. Proving you with a bandaid for the bullet wound. Often they are feeding the idea that more is needed from you, that you should become more than you are. They tell you to *set intentions*. The Buddha would say become intention-less. Become indifferent. Become in harmony with what is, and there, in that state, you will find bliss. It is not what your mind can hear. Your mind has been indoctrinated with doing *more* and becoming *someone*. Everyone is attempting to become someone. The person who steps away from the misery in becoming, the person who finds bliss in the ordinary is much more extraordinary than the person who is still miserable with everything. What is the point of becoming, if you are still miserable? This is all you will find in your efforts to become. More misery.

Instead, become familiar with the words of the Buddha. Not intellectually, not with your knowledge, but in your experience. Or you may remain in misery. These are your options. Remain in misery, fully aware, or in distraction. Or come to realize the potential of bliss. Either way, you will be in search of happiness. In your constant desires for money, beauty, and power, you are looking for bliss that you will never find. Or come to realize that these attempts are futile. Come to desire desirelessness. Come to desire mindlessness. Then drop the mind, and drop all desires and find bliss.

The Buddha said:

Those who follow the way are like unto warriors who fight single-handed with a multitude of foes. They may all go out of the fort in full armor; but among them are some who are faint-hearted, and some who go halfway and beat a retreat, and some who are killed in the affray, and some who come home victorious. O monks, if you desire to attain enlightenment, you should steadily walk in your way, with a resolute heart, with courage, and should be fearless in whatever environment you may happen to be, and destroy every evil influence that you may come across; **for thus you shall reach the goal.**

Learn More

To learn more, visit deveanchase.com for free written content as well as videos in which Devean answers questions from readers like you.

Printed in Great Britain
by Amazon